# Drug Abuse
# In the Workplace:
# An Employer's Guide
# For Prevention

Mark A. de Bernardo

Copyright © 1987

## *Drug Abuse in the Workplace:*
## *An Employer's Guide For Prevention*

Additional copies are available postpaid:

       Single Copy      $15.00 each for members
                       $30.00 each for non-members
       Bulk prices available upon request

Add appropriate sales tax for deliveries in California and the District of Columbia

Make check or money order payable to:
U.S. Chamber of Commerce
1615 H Street, N.W.
Washington, D.C. 20062

or dial direct:
(301) 468-5128
U.S. Chamber Publication #6972

# Notice

Employers' and employees' rights and responsibilities regarding drugs in the workplace are in a constant state of transition. The courts and the legislatures — at the federal, state, and local levels — all are playing a part in shaping the law. Compliance with federal requirements should not be equated with compliance with state and local requirements. Because drug abuse prevention and drug testing programs involve the risk of substantial legal liability when conducted improperly or in violation of federal, state, or local laws, employers are advised to consult with legal counsel and other relevant professionals.

The U.S. Chamber offers these guidelines as a service to its members and other interested parties. This publication is intended only to provide suggested guidelines to employers. They are suggestions only and should be modified to fit the specific capabilities, needs, and conditions of employers and their employees at particular work sites.

---

This publication is designed to provide accurate and authoritative information in regard to the subject matter covered. It is sold with the understanding that the publisher is not engaged in rendering legal, accounting or other professional service. If legal advice or other expert assistance is required, the services of a competent professional person should be sought.

— *From a declaration of principles jointly adopted by a committee of the American Bar Association and a committee of publishers and associations.*

# About the Author

Mark A. de Bernardo is the Special Counsel for Domestic Policy and Manager of Labor Law for the U.S. Chamber of Commerce, where he has served as an attorney since 1979. He is responsible for the Chamber's efforts on drug abuse prevention and labor-management relations.

Mr. de Bernardo represents the interests of the U.S. Chamber's members on these issues before Congress and regulatory and adjudicatory agencies. He testifies often at hearings before Congress and is a frequent guest on television and radio programs. He also writes extensively on labor issues. He is a member of the District of Columbia Bar and is active in the Labor Section of the American Bar Association.

Mr. de Bernardo graduated with honors from Marquette University and the Georgetown University Law Center.

He, his wife Jennifer, and his son Joseph reside in Alexandria, Virginia.

# Table of Contents

## Chapter

## Appendices

# Introduction

Today, in the United States, 5,000 Americans will try cocaine for the first time; nearly 2,000 Americans will be arrested for drug-related crimes; and more than 2,700 boats and planes will smuggle illegal drugs into the country.

American society **does** face a drug abuse epidemic. President Reagan calls drug abuse "our nation's number one problem." Roger Smith, chairman of the board of General Motors, says drug abuse costs GM more than $1 billion a year.

Drug abuse has reached every state, every community, every school district, and virtually every workplace. Drug abuse has reached **your** workplace.

America is losing the war on drugs. Law enforcement officials can't win it alone . . . nor can the government . . . or the schools. It can only be won by a collective effort by all segments of our society.

Do employers have a role in drug abuse prevention? Yes. **The** most effective deterrent to drug abuse is in business' hands — employment. The paycheck is a powerful incentive for employees or prospective employees to stay — or to become — "drug free."

Not only do employers have the means to help decrease drug abuse, they have the incentive: drug abuse costs employers $60 billion a year. The human loss and suffering is incalculable.

This publication is intended to help you understand the price you pay as an employer for employee drug and alcohol abuse . . . and also the costs, and the commitment, it takes to implement an effective corporate program for drug abuse identification, intervention, and prevention.

One employer's experience may be illuminating. Armco's National Supply Company plant in Houston, Texas, undertook a comprehensive drug abuse prevention program. Its results include a two-thirds reduction in its accident rate and a 15 percent increase in productivity. Furthermore, quality is up and turnover down.

1

The first step for every employer is to determine if you have a drug abuse problem of sufficient magnitude to warrant implementation of a corporate response. An effective corporate drug abuse prevention program, comprehensively and fairly administered, requires a major commitment of time and resources.

For most employers, however, the issue is not: "Can you afford it?" The issue is: "Can you afford **not** to do it?"

# Chapter 1

# What They're Saying About Drug Abuse

Quotes from our nation's leaders, drug abuse prevention experts, and concerned business persons tell a story all their own about the magnitude of the drug abuse problem — and the resolve necessary to address it:

"We seek a drug-free workplace — at all levels of government and in the private sector. . . . Those of you in union halls and workplaces everywhere — please make this challenge a part of your job every day. Help us preserve the health and dignity of all workers. To businesses large and small — we need the creativity of your enterprise applied directly to this national problem. Help us."
— *President Ronald Reagan*

"Each of us has to put our principles and consciences on the line — whether in social settings or in the workplace — to set forth solid standards and stick to them. There's no moral middle ground. Indifference is not an option. We want you to help us create an outspoken intolerance for drug use. For the sake of our children, I implore each of you to be unyielding and inflexible in your opposition to drugs."
— *Nancy Reagan*

"If our country does not wake up and address the disastrous and wide-ranging effects of drug abuse in the workplace, the

United States is doomed to become a second-rate power."
— *Dr. Carlton Turner, former Special Assistant to the President for Drug Abuse Policy*

"Drug abuse is an insidious evil. . . . It must be stopped and it will be stopped. . . . I am convinced that the best way and only way is through confidential and professional drug testing."
— *Peter Ueberroth, Commissioner of Baseball*

"Our message is simple — If you do drugs, you don't work. This is not a role that business people seek or enjoy, but it is ours whether we like it or not. We have no alternative but to commit ourselves to this cause [drug abuse prevention] and to see it through."
— *Dr. Richard L. Lesher, President, U.S. Chamber of Commerce*

"The workplace is literally riddled with substance abusers, both on and off the job. . . . What should employers do? The first step is to develop a clear policy on drugs and alcohol, and to ensure that this policy is effectively communicated to all employees and fully supported by top management."
— *Peter Bensinger, President, Bensinger, DuPont, and Associates, former administrator, U.S. Drug Enforcement Administration*

"If . . . business continues as it has in the last year to develop more and more stringent kinds of policies, it eventually will reduce the demand for illicit substances. It may be very effective in changing the way people view drug taking in this country. . . . I believe in my own mind that there is a healthy segment of the population that would like to have a reason for saying 'no thanks.' "

— *Dr. Michael Walsh, National Institute on Drug Abuse*

"Every employer, public and private, and public education institutions at all levels should have clearly stated policies prohibiting drug use, possession of drugs, or being under the influence of drugs on the premises. The consequences of violating these prohibitions should be clearly explained. Government and private sector employers who do not already require drug testing of job applicants and current employees should consider the appropriateness of such a testing program."

— *'America's Habit: Drug Abuse, Drug Trafficking and Organized Crime,' Report of the President's Commission on Organized Crime, March 1986*

"Job-based interventions . . . are usually justified in the minds of most drug abusers and those who work around them . . . the workplace has the power to intervene. . . . The workplace more than other 'places' [the family, the courts, or the churches], has the personnel . . . to effect an intervention, to monitor it, and the resources to develop contacts with appropriate treatment opportunities in the community."

— *Harrison Trice, Professor of Industrial and Labor Relations, Cornell University*

"We have a right to say how you behave at the workplace. You don't bring a gun to work. You can't come to work naked. You're not allowed to yell 'fire' in the middle of the factory. We're just asking people to be fit while they're on the job."

— *Peter Cherry, Cherry Electrical Products*

"I consider drugs damn dangerous. I believe that my responsibility is such that my position against drugs has to be clearly understood by everyone who works under my direction."
— *Daniel Burke, President, Capital Cities/ABC*

"We do a lot of highly classified work here, and people with these problems [drug abuse] are much higher security risks [because they are vulnerable to blackmail]."
— *R. Richard Heppe, President, Lockheed California*

"You can no longer assume that because a person wears a three-piece suit and a necktie, you can rule out drug abuse."
— *Naomi Behrman, AT&T/Bell Labs*

"We're not on a witch hunt. Our number one concern here is safety. We also have a responsibility to our customers."
— *John Hunt, Personnel Manager, Southern California Edison*

"Our purpose is to make sure we have the safety, security, and performance required in the company's operations. Our goal is to have an environment free of drug abuse."
— *Sam Egbert, General Electric*

"Many jobs in our industry can be quite difficult or dangerous if performed by people whose perception, judgment, and reactions are impaired or influenced by illegal use of drugs."
— *Arthur Bentley, UNOCAL*

"Many employers say the problem doesn't exist, but it does, and we have to deal with it. . . . Cocaine is the biggest problem. Then it's grass, pills, and alcohol. Cocaine is not the rich man's drug any-

more; it's the working man's drug too. . . .
We tell supervisors that it's not their place
to get involved in an employer's personal
life, but they can and should be involved
with productivity and job performance."
— *Robert Harris, Director of Corporate
Loss Prevention, United Grocers,
Inc.*

"When you deal with the public, cour-
tesy, kindness, good habits are crucial. If
someone I hire is strung out or has a bad
habit, he takes it to work with him.
Though I don't deal in life or death situations, as far as my business goes, it's life
or death for me, a livelihood that could be
compromised."
— *Eugene King, Vice President of a
freight company San Antonio, Texas*

"We're concerned about performance.
We're concerned about the effects of alcohol, but I can tell from someone's be-
haviour if they come to work drunk. Not
so with drugs. About 80 percent of performance problems from drugs are invis-
ible. I equate our concern with that of the
airline industry. When you walk on a
plane, you don't want pilots to just appear
drug-free. You want to be absolutely sure
they are. . . . Drug use can exert financial
demands — temptations — we don't want
on employees."
— *Edwin Weihenmayer, Vice President
and Director of Human Resources,
Kidder, Peabody & Co.*

"The threat of losing a job seems to be
the most effective means of getting a person to face the problem [of drug abuse]."
— *Jim McGregor, Public Relations Director, Bath Iron Works*

"I think if your private affairs interfere
with society, we [employers] do have a

right [to implement drug testing], especially if it's [drug abuse] something that once you start, you can't control. One way or the other, your drug use is going to become my business."

*— Bud Musell, Personnel Manager of a retail company, La Fayette, N.Y.*

"We have a responsibility to stockholders and employees to provide the best and safest working environment. With someone using drugs, there is less productivity, less creativity. I don't think we can legislate morality, but we can put together the best team possible."

*— Jerry Fields, Director of Safety and Health, Boise Cascade*

"Why should the social and economic burden of drug users be imposed on corporations? They must compete and make a profit. If one corporation screens out drug users, it will have a lower accident rate and greater productivity, while a company that doesn't screen will be out of business."

*— Dr. William Hsiao, Professor, Harvard School of Public Health*

"A lot of my old friends are dead."
*— A rehabilitating cocaine abuser as quoted in* Time *magazine*

# Chapter 2

# The Drug User As Employee

Workers who use drugs illegally greatly compromise their performance. Compared with average employee rates, a typical "recreational" drug user in today's work force is:

- 2.2 times more likely to request early dismissal or time off,

- 2.5 times more likely to have absences of eight days or more,

*drugs' effects on workers*

- 3 times more likely to be late for work,

- 3.6 times more likely to injure themselves or another person in a workplace accident,

- 5 times more likely to be involved in an accident **off** the job (which, in turn, affects attendance or performance **on** the job),

- 5 times more likely to file a workers' compensation claim,

- 7 times more likely to have wage garnishments, and

- One-third less productive.

Furthermore, drug-abusing employees incur 300 percent higher medical costs and benefits.

There also are substantial, but difficult to calculate precisely, additional costs: lower morale, decreased quality of products or services, absenteeism for family members of drug abusers, destruction of company property, higher insurance rates, stolen money or property from the company or co-workers, and impaired judgment regarding everyday decisions affecting the company. The effects — negative effects — of drug abuse on the workplace are pervasive.

*"hidden" costs*

A recent survey of drug users who were seeking help in regard to their drug habits revealed that:

- 75 percent said they had used drugs on the job,

- 64 percent admitted drugs had adversely affected job performance,

*use on the job*

- 44 percent said they had sold drugs to other employees, and

- 18 percent said they had stolen from co-workers to support their habits.

# Chapter 3

# Extent of the Drug Abuse Problem

One corporate executive recently said: "We don't assume that we have a greater [drug] problem than **the nation as a whole.** But we decided that we couldn't stick our heads in the sand."

"The nation as a whole" has an immense drug problem. If your employer, your employees, your company had a drug problem that is "only" average for American society, you have serious trouble. The business community — and all of us as individuals — can ill afford to "stick our heads in the sand." Drug abuse is a problem that must be addressed more effectively soon.

Drug abuse is a growing national concern — and for good reason. We all should recognize the magnitude of our nation's drug abuse problem:

(1) **65 percent** of those persons entering the full-time work force for the first time have experience in illegal drug use; **42 percent** in the last year.

*extent of drug use*

(2) **23 million** Americans use marijuana on a regular basis (at least four times a month); **6 million** Americans use cocaine on a regular basis.

(3) **10 million** Americans use prescription drugs without an appropriate medical prescription.

(4) **500,000** Americans are addicted to heroin.

(5) As many as **23 percent** of all U.S. workers use dangerous drugs on the job.

(6) **22 million** Americans have used cocaine at least occasionally, **4.2 million** in the last month. Furthermore, **three-quarters** of those calling the cocaine "hotline" said they sometimes took cocaine on the job; **one-quarter** said they used cocaine on the job daily.

(7) **$60 billion** is the annual cost to the business community for drug abuse, a **30 percent** increase in only three years. **$35 billion** of that cost is in lost productivity.

*cost of drug use*

(8) **60 percent** of the world's production of illegal drugs is consumed in the United States — a fact that has obvious ramifications on U.S. international competitiveness.

(9) **One-in-four** narcotics users sells drugs to co-workers, friends, and neighbors to support a drug habit.

(10) **More than one million** legally manufactured doses of drugs were stolen in the United States last year.

(11) **708,400** suspects were arrested on drug charges in 1984, and arrest rates are increasing.

*drug-related arrests*

(12) Cocaine deaths **doubled** from 1981 to 1985; deaths attributable to drug overdoses increased by **93 percent** in only four years (1979–1983).

*drug-related deaths*

(13) **12 tons** of heroin, **65 tons** of marijuana, and **150 tons** of cocaine were distributed in the United States in 1986.

(14) **More than $110 billion** is grossed annually from the illegal sale of drugs in the United States — more than the total American farmers take in from all crops and more than double the combined profits of all Fortune 500 companies.

(15) The **third largest** cash crop in the United States is marijuana.

(16) A study of nearly 250 drug addicts over an 11-year period found that an **average 1,946 crimes** were committed by the addicts.

(17) Case studies of drug addicts have found that they spent as much as **$6,000 per week** to support their drug habits.

(18) **More than two-thirds** of the 26,000 people who sought counseling for cocaine addiction in 1985 failed to be rehabilitated.

(19) *USA Today* reported in March 1986 that **77 percent** of those persons polled in a recent survey said they would not object to being tested in the workplace for drugs.

(20) **Between 65 and 80 percent** of drug abuse problems would be resolved by a drug abuse prevention program that includes drug testing, according to some estimates (because of deterrence for social users and rehabilitation for chronic users).

Some estimates regarding the extent of the drug abuse problem vary. However, **all** estimates can lead to only one conclusion: Drug abuse in the United States is a severe problem.

# Chapter 4

# Employer Guidelines for a Workplace Drug Abuse Prevention Program

Drug abuse costs American business more than $60 billion a year in lost productivity, increased absenteeism, workplace accidents, rising medical costs and theft.

The U.S. Chamber strongly supports a drug-free workplace. Employer strategies to achieve this goal should include some or all of the following:

- commitment to a drug-free workplace
- policy development
- education, training, and communication
- enforcement
- drug testing
- rehabilitation
- disciplinary action
- follow-up

The U.S. Chamber offers these guidelines as an aid to employers who are considering the implementation of a drug abuse prevention program. Note: The priority actions are noted with asterisks.

## COMMITMENT

*commitment*

(1)* **Commit** your firm at the **senior management** level to a drug-free workplace.

(2) **Review** the records of employees with drug abuse problems (if any), and **decide** whether your company has a **drug abuse problem** significant enough to warrant a formal program.

(3) **Analyze personnel and productivity records** for abnormal increases in absenteeism, accidents, compensation claims, turnover, thefts of company property, grievance proceedings, wage garnishments, and employee arrests, **or** for abnormal decreases in production deadlines and goals being met. Any such entries may indicate drug abuse. Consult with supervisors and employee representatives regarding their analyses of the extent of the problem. This procedure should be repeated periodically as needed.

(4)* **Decide** whether **drug testing** will be a part of the company's program and when, how, and **for whom** drug testing will be administered (e.g., job applicants, all employees, employees in jobs involving safety or security, employees who have had accidents, whether testing will be periodic and announced or random and unannounced).

*policy development*

(5) **Determine** what **disciplinary measures** (e.g., dismissal, suspension, demotion, transfer) will be taken against employees who violate the company's drug abuse prevention policy.

(6) **Recognize** that **alcohol abuse and illegal use of prescription drugs** are major drug abuse problems and **need**

to be addressed comprehensively as well.

(7) **Estimate the costs** of employee assistance and rehabilitation programs as they relate to **health insurance, workers' compensation,** and **unemployment compensation.**

(8) **Draft** a preliminary **company policy** on drug abuse in the workplace.

(9) **Coordinate** your company's policy and program **internally in the company** with those individuals responsible for labor relations, personnel, legal counsel, medical care, security, public affairs, and occupational safety and health.

*coordinate policy*

(10) **Contact local experts** on crime prevention, medicine, and rehabilitation and counseling services: (a) for their recommendations; (b) as a source of expertise; and (c) as a contact for future referrals.

(11)* **Inform** your **union or employee association** representatives (if there are any) of your company's policy and program, and enlist their cooperation and support.

(12)* **Issue** a **formal written company policy** statement on drug abuse in the workplace that explains: (a) the company's commitment to a drug-free workplace; (b) under what circumstances (if at all) drug testing will be conducted; (c) the consequences of refusal to participate in drug testing; (d) the consequences of violation of the company's drug abuse prevention policy; and (e) that law enforcement officials will be contacted when appropriate with respect to the use, sale, purchase, or possession of illegal drugs on the job is confirmed.

## EDUCATION, TRAINING, AND COMMUNICATION

(13)   **Communicate** your **policy to employees** through: (a) briefings; (b) notices in company newsletters, in paycheck envelopes, and on company bulletin boards; and (c) letters from the company president or plant manager.

*communication*

(14)   **Inform** employees of the **reasons for** the company's anti-drug abuse **policy,** recognizing that the success of the program is dependent upon its acceptance by the employees and job applicants themselves.

(15)*   **Make being "drug free" a condition of employment, informing job applicants** that employment is contingent on applicants and employees being free of drugs. Establish this policy through statements on job applications and in employee handbooks.

(16)   **Apply,** to the extent permissible and appropriate, **company policies to temporary or subcontractor employees** when they are on company premises. This includes temporary secretarial, security, delivery, and janitorial personnel. Provide notice to both the employees and their employers.

(17)*   **Educate** employees about the **dangers of drug abuse** using: (a) lectures by experts in the community; (b) films; (c) brochures; and (d) fact sheets to **stress prevention** of drug

*education*

18

abuse through drug education and awareness.

(18) **Designate a contact person** with whom employees can discuss drug abuse concerns regarding themselves or their fellow workers; inform employees of how, where, and when this person can be reached; and make this contact person regularly and readily available. Keep the **lines of communication open** and recognize the importance of employee suggestions and feedback to the company's drug abuse prevention program.

(19) **Require employees** in jobs that involve safety or security who legally are **using prescription drugs** for medical conditions, and for whom those drugs could impair their performance, either to register with the appropriate medical or personnel office and/or **to notify their supervisors.**

(20) **Train supervisors** how to: (a) **detect the symptoms** of drug abuse; (b) **identify illegal drugs** and drug paraphernalia; and (c) **respond to crisis situations** such as receiving reports of illegal drugs in plain view or being confronted by an employee who is obviously under the influence of drugs and may need to be restrained or medically assisted.

*training*

(21) **Inform** local **police authorities** of your program and cooperate regarding criminal investigations.

(22) **Support community drug abuse prevention programs** to: (a) demonstrate to employees and the public your company's commit-

ment to the "war on drugs"; and (b) assume a positive civic responsibility — including involvement in, support of, and contributions to drug education and awareness programs at local schools and colleges.

## ENFORCEMENT

(23) **Show full support for supervisors.** This will: (a) demonstrate the commitment to, and seriousness of, the company's anti-drug abuse policy; (b) assure supervisors and employees that they should cooperate in efforts to identify those employees who violate the law and the company's policy; and (c) deter further violations.

*supervisors*

(24) **Discipline supervisors** who, in administering and enforcing the company's drug abuse prevention program, abuse their power, harass employees, lie, or otherwise act in bad faith. Employees must be shown that the company's drug abuse prevention program is fair and consistent in order to assure meaningful cooperation and maintain positive morale.

(25) **Maintain thorough, secure, and confidential records** not only for drug test results, but also for drug-related accidents or incidents. The best defense to a legal challenge to disciplinary action based on drug abuse — and an important safeguard for protecting innocent employees — is documentation.

(26)* **Enforce the company policy consistently.** Be prepared to make the same response when a "positive" drug test is confirmed for a long-

*even enforcement*

term, highly placed employee as for a newly hired employee whose performance is marginal.

(27)  **Use discretion** in employing: (a) locker, office, or vehicle searches; (b) hidden cameras; (c) undercover operations; (d) dogs trained to detect drugs, or other vigorous **surveillance and detection techniques.** Implement such techniques only **when necessary** to address severe drug selling or abuse problems in the workplace.

## DRUG TESTING

(28)  **Remember,** if implemented, **drug testing is only one aspect** of a comprehensive strategy to prevent drug abuse in the workplace.

(29)  **Contract** with a reliable, **professional drug-testing service** — or use an in-house testing program — that will assure quality control and chain-of-custody for test samples. In addition, stress that personnel are trained and that the manufacturer's instructions for the testing apparatus are followed to the letter. It also is advisable to use a service that has professionals qualified and available to serve as expert witnesses if necessary.

*drug testing*

(30)*  **Implement drug testing** in as fairly, accurately, and legally defensible a manner as is reasonable considering your company's individual situation. Extreme caution must be used to assure that the collection, handling, and testing procedures are reliable and accurate, and to prevent misidentification. Extreme caution also must be used because relevant laws are constantly changing and require consultation with legal counsel before implementation.

(31)* **Request** — not require — job applicants at the time the drug test is administered to sign a **waiver** of legal rights of action against the employer. As a legal protection, this waiver permits the test and waives the employee's right to challenge the ability of the employer to administer the test or act on the test's results. Such releases of employer liability, signed at the time of hire, must be signed knowingly and willingly.

*waiver forms*

(32) **Split** the **specimen** taken for urinalysis into **two samples,** so that a second test can be performed using the same specimen when the first half of that specimen tests "positive" for drug presence.

*split specimens*

(33) **Perform confirmation assays** when the first half of an employee's sample tests "positive" before taking disciplinary action, making sure that a **different chemical process** — such as gas chromatography/mass spectrometry — is used for the confirming drug test than was used for the initial drug test to assure reliability.

*confirmation tests*

(34) **Retain "positive"** test **samples** as evidence, maintaining refrigerated preservation of samples for a reasonable length of time as a legal precaution.

(35) **Preserve** the **confidentiality** of drug test results, making every effort to observe reasonable employee expectations of privacy and confidentiality.

(36) **Provide** timely and complete notification to employees who test and retest "positive" for drugs, informing them of the **drug test results** and what they mean.

## REHABILITATION

(37)* **Provide** the opportunity — **when feasible** and appropriate — for employees who test "positive" to participate in company-sponsored employee assistance and **rehabilitation programs.** These programs should include medical monitoring, treatment, retesting, and counseling. Recognize that the identification of a drug abuse problem is only the first step and that rehabilitation is the ultimate and most humane goal.

*Employee Assistance Programs*

(38) **Provide referrals to local counseling and treatment centers** for employees with drug abuse problems as an alternative to, or as a supplement for, company employee assistance programs.

(39) **Insist** on a high level of **accountability for employees in** company-sponsored or company-referred **drug rehabilitation programs.** Make such programs available only to those employees who acknowledge the existence of a drug abuse problem. Stress that strict adherence to the requirements of the program and random retesting are the only alternative to dismissal for employees with a drug abuse problem.

*account-
ability*

(40) **Address** the **family and dependent problems** of employees who are drug abusers with emphasis on group,

family, personal, and outpatient counseling.

## DISCIPLINARY ACTION

(41) **Document** as fully as possible a relationship between **declining job performance** and drug abuse before taking disciplinary action against employees. This is especially important for employees in jobs where there is either: (a) minimal risk to the safety of the public or co-workers; (b) little need for public trust; or (c) no access to substantial amounts of cash or valuables.

*job performance*

(42)* **Dismiss** those **employees with chronic drug abuse problems** who: (a) are unable or unwilling to rehabilitate; (b) pose a significant safety or security risk; (c) are unable to perform the duties of the job for which they were hired due to impairment or incapacity caused by illegal drug use; or (d) have been apprehended selling drugs illegally on the job.

*dismissal*

(43) **Establish a mechanism for** a quick and fair **review of employee complaints** and resolution of grievances filed by employees who are discharged, suspended, demoted, or transferred for violation of the company's drug abuse prevention policy.

## FOLLOW–UP

(44) **Monitor legislative and legal developments** regarding relevant: (a) federal, state, and local legislation; (b) National Labor Relations Board decisions; (c) arbitration awards; and (d) court decisions regarding the employment-at-will

doctrine and its relationship to employees discharged for on-the-job drug abuse. Revise your company's drug abuse prevention program accordingly.

(45) **Evaluate** — periodically and at a senior management level — **how well the company's objectives are being achieved** by your drug abuse prevention program and policies. Make **changes where necessary** and appropriate.

*evaluation*

# Chapter 5

# Reacting to a Workplace Drug Incident: A Supervisor's Checklist

Be prepared to act on a workplace drug abuse problem. Supervisors should **know** what to do when confronted with an employee under the influence of drugs or otherwise in clear violation of the company's drug abuse prevention policy.

The following suggestions should help supervisors when confronted with a drug abuse situation:

*how to react to a workplace problem*

- Make sure reliable witnesses are present. **Never** take action alone.

- Have security personnel on notice and available if necessary.

- Notify immediate supervisors and the plant or office manager.

- Confront the employee, announce your suspicions, and request an explanation.

- Confiscate any suspected drugs and related items (e.g., pipes or syringes). Give employees a receipt for whatever materials are taken.

- Ask the employee to take a drug screening test. Have the test administered as soon as possible after you suspect a problem.

- Suspend the employee (with or without pay, according to company policy), pending the outcome of a formal investigation.

27

- Advise the employee not to drive when leaving work if under the influence of drugs.

- Discharge or suspend the employee immediately, according to company policy, if the employee: (a) refuses to take a drug test; (b) insists on driving home while impaired; or (c) is excessively hostile or threatening.

- Call police or other law enforcement authorities immediately if weapons are confiscated or present, or if the confiscated property is found to be an illegal substance of the nature and quantity warranting police involvement in your jurisdiction.

- Prepare a detailed written report of what occurred as soon after the incident as possible.

# Chapter 6

# What Not to Do

What you **don't** do in your drug abuse prevention program can be as important as what you do:

- **Don't** misuse the drug abuse prevention program to discipline employees for other purposes (e.g., to discharge an employee because of substandard performance).

- **Don't** concentrate testing, searches, or other enforcement actions on any one class of employees. Be especially careful not to concentrate your efforts — even unintentionally — on any of the "protected" classes under the equal employment laws (e.g., race, sex, or religion). Too much attention to any one group could result in charges of discrimination.

- **Don't** confront a suspected drug user one-on-one. This can be dangerous physically and can weaken management's position legally.

- **Don't** assume supervisors and other management employees do not or cannot have a drug abuse problem.

- **Don't** implement a verbal policy. A truly effective drug abuse prevention policy is set, in writing, and communicated to employees.

- **Don't** treat workers who test "positive" for drugs differently — discharging some workers while only suspending or warning others.

*what not to do*

- **Don't** take disciplinary action against **employees** — except in extraordinary circumstances — based on the results of only one drug test. Always confirm a "positive" test using a different chemical process on a split sample of a single specimen. For **job applicants,** the results of a single drug test, in certain circumstances, may be considered sufficient to deny employment, absent a credible explanation (such as treatment for a medical condition). However, confirmation using a split sample of a single specimen also is recommended for job applicants.

- **Don't** provide rehabilitation services selectively.

- **Don't** address drug abuse in the workplace without also implementing a parallel program on alcohol abuse.

- **Don't** act without notifying your union (if any), and **don't** refuse to bargain over your drug abuse prevention program. The National Labor Relations Act requires employers whose employees are represented by a union to bargain not only on wages and hours, but also on terms and conditions of employment. Drug testing is within these parameters, unless a broad "management rights" provision is in the collective bargaining agreement and can be interpreted to allow you to implement a program without union approval. Nonetheless, cooperative efforts are preferable to unilateral action.

- **Don't** lose sight of the ultimate goal of a drug abuse prevention program — rehabilitation.

# Chapter 7

# Ten Questions And Answers About Drug Testing

(1) **How extensive is drug testing?**

Very extensive and increasing all the time. In 1983, only 3 percent of the Fortune 500 companies had drug testing programs. By 1986, the number had risen to more than 30 percent. By the end of 1987, the number will exceed 50 percent. Although less common for small- and medium-sized businesses, drug testing nonetheless is widespread even among these employers.

*how extensive*

The companies with drug testing programs for job applicants and/or employees include: Unocal, IBM, Kodak, DuPont, *The New York Times*, the American Broadcasting Company/Capital Cities, General Motors, United Airlines, USAir, Lockheed, and General Electric.

(2) **Why are employers interested in drug testing?**

Employers are interested in drug abuse prevention, not just drug testing. Drug testing — for **some** employment situations — can be an effective component of a drug abuse prevention program. It is not an answer in itself. It **may** be part of the answer.

The human and financial cost of drug abuse in the workplace is enormous. Employers want to protect their employees, customers, and the public at large from the higher rate of accidents that drug abuse causes. Employers also want to protect their investments and their profits. Employees with drugs in their systems are only two-thirds as productive as drug-free employees. The cost of drug abuse **to employers** is $60 billion annually.

*why businesses are testing*

Finally, employers want to address the drug abuse epidemic that plagues our society because it is a national concern and because they feel they have a responsibility to the community to do their part to prevent drug abuse. They know **the** most effective deterrent to drug abuse may be contingency of employment — your job depending on your being drug-free.

(3) **What type of drug testing is usually used?**

The most common types of drug testing involve urinalysis. A urine specimen is taken from the person being tested. That specimen subsequently is mixed at a lab with a chemical that reacts to a specific drug. Tests can be programmed to detect the presence of marijuana, cocaine, heroin, and a variety of other illegal — or legal — drugs.

*type of drug tests*

Generally, drug testing is most effective, equitable, and accurate when it involves a two-step process with two different testing methods.

The first step is initial screening, a relatively simple and inexpensive procedure. EMIT, manufactured by Syntex Corporation, and ABUSCREEN, manufactured by Roche Diagnostics, are the two most widely used initial screening tests, both using immunoassay techniques. This is followed by a second, confirming test, usually performed on the second portion of an original sample using a different chemical process. The most common method of confirmation is a gas chromatography/mass spectrometry test.

(4) **How reliable is drug testing?**

Initial drug screening tests may result in some "false positives" or "false negatives." But the range of accuracy for the most common initial drug screening tests is between 92 and 98 percent.

*reliability*

Furthermore, a two-step program that includes a confirmation assay is as certain in its results as is technologically possible when administered properly. The gas chromatography/mass spectrometry test alone is virtually without any margin of error.

(5) **What can be done to assure accuracy?**

Human error is the most common reason for inaccuracies in testing today. Thus, an employer should take every precaution to ensure the integrity of its drug testing program.

*preventing human error*

Some of the ways to assure accuracy include: (1) using well-trained and certified personnel who will follow acceptable professional procedures; (2) assuring chain-of-custody for specimens so that tampering, substitution, misidentification, or misplacement will not occur; (3) splitting initial specimens into two samples so that a second test can be performed using the **initial** specimen when the first half of that specimen tests "positive" for drug presence; and (4) performing the second test using a different chemical process, called a confirmation assay. The most common confirming tests are: gas chromatography/ mass spectrometry, gas chromatography, or high performance liquid chromatography.

(6) **Can passive inhalation of marijuana smoke lead to a "positive" urinalysis?**

Highly unlikely. Inadvertent exposure to marijuana smoke is sometimes claimed to be the cause of a "positive" drug test. But according to the National Institute on Drug Abuse: "Clinical studies have shown . . . that it is highly unlikely that a nonsmoking individual could inhale sufficient smoke by passive inhalation to result in a high enough drug concentration in urine for detection at the cutoff of currently used urinalysis methods."

(7) **How long do drugs stay in the system after use?**

For 96–97 percent of the people, detectable levels of marijuana stay in the body for 2–5 days after use. For chronic users of marijuana, retention can be much longer — as high as several weeks, but only in extreme situations. To retain any trace of marijuana in the body more than five days after use requires a massive, constant, cumulative intake.

*body retention of drugs*

Cocaine stays in the system for 2–3 days after use.

(8) **Is it legal for employers to make being "drug free" a condition of employment for job applicants?**

Yes. There is no federal or state constitutional provision that directly prohibits drug screening programs. Some laws affect an employer's ability to test **employees,** but an employer clearly has a strong right to implement a drug testing program for **job applicants.** Since job applicants are not employees, they do not have employees' rights.

Employers have a **right** to make being drug free a condition of employment. In certain industries — especially those involving public safety or security — employers may be considered to have a **duty** to assure that their work force is drug free. A prime example of such a work force is airline pilots.

Job applicants, of course, do have a choice. They can choose to work elsewhere. Generally, refusal to submit to a drug test will result in denial of employment for job applicants.

Being drug free is as legally justifiable a condition of employment as a requirement to take a physical, provide references, or have a level of education or English language ability necessary to the performance of the job.

(9) **Don't employees have a right to privacy?**

Yes. Individual rights, privacy, and confidentiality are valid concerns. For that reason, employers should use discretion, minimize intrusions, and be sensitive and responsive to individuals' concerns.

However, individual rights need to be balanced against the interests of effectively combatting the drug abuse epidemic. The public safety, efficient performance, product integrity, and employee morale are all valid interests as well. The common good must be kept in focus, even if it temporarily — but reasonably — inconveniences or offends some individuals.

*employee privacy*

Recent polls have demonstrated that a vast majority of workers have **no** objection to being tested for drugs. The average American recognizes the threat that drug abuse poses not only to our workplaces, but to our families. They recognize the magnitude of the drug abuse problem and the valid role employers have to play in addressing it.

(10) **What are the penalties for people who test "positive" for drugs?**

For **job applicants,** the penalty invariably is denial of employment.

For **employees,** the responses of companies to "positive" drug tests are more diverse. Confirmation is essential. Second tests using a different chemical process should be employed. Only if both tests are "positive," should an employer take action.

But what action? The options for serious drug abuse problems include: (1) suspending the employee, **with** pay, pending successful rehabilitation efforts; (2) suspending the employee, **without** pay, pending successful

*employer options*

rehabilitation efforts; or (3) dismissal. The first option is the most humane; the last may be the most effective for deterrence. Of course, another employer option for those employees with less severe drug problems who are in non-critical jobs is simply to require the employee to undergo rehabilitation while continuing to work.

*rehabilitation*

However, employers should keep in mind that the ultimate goal in identifying employees with drug abuse problems is **rehabilitation.** Toward that end, company-sponsored employee assistance programs, referral to public counseling and rehabilitation centers, and reasonable efforts to offer continued employment are appropriate and advisable.

# Chapter 8

# Drug Testing: When and Who to Test

An employer who decides to implement a drug abuse prevention program — and to include drug testing as part of that program — also must decide when and who to test. The employer's options include:

## (1) Job Applicant Drug Screening

Job applicants are by far the **most common** group of persons to be tested by employers for drugs. Virtually all employers who require any drug testing, require it for job applicants. The ratio of companies requiring drug tests for job applicants to companies requiring routine drug tests for employees is probably more than 10-to-1.

*job applicants*

Why are drug tests for job applicants so much more common than drug tests for employees?

One reason is the testing of job applicants is **more legally defensible** than the testing of employees. Of course, job applicants retain the right to refuse to be tested and to seek employment elsewhere. However, employers do have the right to make being "drug-free" a condition of employment for all job applicants prior to being hired.

Furthermore, drug testing for job applicants, unlike for current employees, is not complicated by issues of job performance, benefits, pensions, or severance pay. Job applicant drug testing also is less likely to prompt union grievances or adversely affect employee morale.

Job applicant drug tests are considered cost-effective because they are most likely to have a preventive impact on drug-related workplace problems. By keeping drug users off the job, costly problems involving safety, absenteeism, and productivity can be avoided altogether.

Finally, drug testing for job applicants is most likely to deter drug use by young people entering the work force — the age group for whom drug use is most prevalent — because it communicates a consistent and established anti-drug abuse policy at the outset of their job searches.

## (2) Drug Testing Based on Safety Concerns

Much less common, but still defensible from a legal standpoint, is the administration of drug tests for employees in jobs involving the safety of the employee, co-workers, and the public, or the protection of persons and property. The transportation, construction, and utilities industries are primary examples.

*tests in the interests of safety*

The potential liabilities an employer faces for **not** assuring a safe and secure working environment are one incentive. Another is the legal doctrine that upholds such drug testing based on a compelling public interest when personal rights and public safety are in conflict. Can **anyone** doubt that a subway conductor, bulldozer operator, or nuclear reactor employee needs to be "drug free"?

### (3) "For Cause" Drug Testing

Employee drug testing "for cause" also is increasing.

Such tests are common as part of a post-accident investigation when human error may have been involved.

*incident-driven*

Tests also may be incident-driven as part of an investigation when a specific event indicates a potential employee drug abuse problem. For example, when illegal drugs are observed at an employee's work station or there is evidence that an employee's declining job performance is drug-related, an employer's response may include drug testing.

### (4) Post-Treatment Drug Testing

It also is common — and appropriate — for employees who have acknowledged drug abuse problems and have participated in drug rehabilitation programs to be retested.

*retests*

Their continued employment often is conditioned on their successful rehabilitation, a rehabilitation which is demonstrated by their testing "negative" for drugs. While drug abuse is a disease that sometimes is difficult to identify, rehabilitation may be equally difficult to assure — if there is no effective retesting for the presence of drugs.

Failure to submit to retests is generally considered an appropriate basis for dismissal or denial of reinstatement of employees with drug abuse problems.

### (5) Periodic, Announced Drug Testing

Perhaps the business community's first experience with drug testing is as part of routine employee medical examinations. Many employers have had standing policies that require physicals for employees, usually on an annual basis.

This is particularly true for employees in jobs that involve stress, require physical endurance, or are at a policymaking level.

*periodic tests*

Because they are scheduled in advance and uniformly administered, such tests are generally more accepted by employees than random, unannounced drug tests.

(6) **Random, Unannounced Drug Tests**

Unannounced employee drug tests, because of their "surprise" nature, are more likely than announced tests to identify those employees who have used drugs illegally.

However, unannounced drug tests — most often performed on a random basis so as not to become predictable — also are the type of employee drug tests most likely to result in employee resentment and legal challenges. A surprise, random drug test may be viewed as arbitrary and offensive, even to those workers who are most opposed to illegal drug use.

*random tests*

Random, unannounced drug tests also are the type of drug testing most likely to trigger union grievances when the work force is unionized. In a nonunion work force, this practice can strengthen the position of the union organizer.

Although random, unannounced drug tests are the least legally defensible of the drug testing options listed, they clearly are by no means indefensible. However, such testing may only be appropriate when a workplace drug abuse problem is pervasive and deep-rooted.

Random, unannounced drug testing is an employer option that should be exercised with great caution, and only after an employer has analyzed the magnitude of the problem and the ramifications of such a response.

# Chapter 9

# Examples of Drug–Related
# Workplace Accidents

The worst-case scenario for drug abuse in the workplace is drug-related accidents that result in loss of life. An employee with drugs in his or her system — not "high," just with drugs in the system — is 3.6 times more likely to injure himself or herself or another person in an accident on the job.

The results can be tragic:

*fatal accidents*

• A railroad employee, high on marijuana while at a train's controls, ignored a stop signal and crashed into the rear of another train in Royersford, Pennsylvania. Two people were killed and damages totaled $467,500.

• At Newark airport, two crewmen were killed when their cargo flight crash-landed. The National Transportation Safety Board attributed the fatal crash to illegal drug use — an autopsy showed that the pilot had been smoking marijuana, possibly while flying.

• A 31-year-old miner was crushed to death by his own truck while high on marijuana and PCP. Two other employees were injured in the drug-related accident.

The record of the railroad industry alone tells the story. Between 1975 and 1984, 48 railroad accidents were caused by drug- or alcohol-impaired workers, according to the Federal Railroad Administration. These wrecks killed 37 people, injured 80 people, and resulted in $34 million in damages, excluding third-party damages.

The loss of life and property is not only substantial, it is also unnecessary. Of course, drug abuse on the job does not always result in fatal or injurious accidents. In fact, no accident at all occurs most of the time. However, the examples mentioned are just three of the thousands of drug-related accidents that occur at workplaces each year.

Some are tragic. Others are just costly.

A computer operator who was high on marijuana cost a major airline $19 million with just one oversight. The computer operator failed to load a crucial tape into the airline's computerized reservations system resulting in eight hours of "down" time. An airline spokesman, commenting on the $19 million loss, said: "That was an awfully expensive joint by anybody's standards."

*computer losses*

A computer operator is considered by some to be a non-hazardous job for which drug testing would be inappropriate. Marijuana is considered by some to be a "soft" drug, not particularly harmful, and beyond what should be the concerns of employers.

Perhaps the airline with the $19 million loss caused by marijuana use would disagree.

# Chapter 10

# Spotting a
# Drug Abuse Problem

A workplace accident kills an employee and seriously injures several others. The accident was caused by an employee who was under the influence of drugs.

Should the employer have known? Was there any advance notice of a problem? How can an employer tell when an employee is "high" on the job?

There are early warning signs . . . but an employer has to know what to look for:

(1) **Drug Paraphernalia**

*the
instruments
of
drug use*

Would your supervisors associate the instruments of drug abuse with a drug problem? False bottom cans, glassine envelopes, medicine droppers, bent teaspoons, crudely wrapped cigarette butts, cigarette "rolling" papers, razor blades, small metal pipes or larger glass "water pipes," and metal "roach" clips all indicate possible illegal drug use.

(2) **Suspicious Behavior**

Unusual incidents on the job also may be an indication of an employee drug abuse problem. An employee who frequently goes to the parking lot during breaks, visits the washroom, makes secretive phone calls, receives unusual packages or deliveries, is visited by strangers or workers from other work areas, dresses inappropriately for the season, or wears sunglasses indoors

**may** be an employee with a drug problem.

Of course, there are other plausible explanations for such behavior. Nonetheless, these activities may provide a warning sign of a drug problem. For example, addicts who wear long sleeve shirts in hot weather may be trying to conceal "needle marks" on their arms, a drug user who wears sunglasses indoors may be trying to hide bloodshot or dilated eyes, or a person who wears or carries a coat in summer may be trying to hide drugs.

(3) **Physical Symptoms of Drug Abuse**

Bloodshot or dilated eyes and "needle marks" are not the only physical symptoms of drug abuse of which an employer should be aware. Slurred speech, delayed reactions, chills in summer, sweating in winter, a continuing nasal infection or congestion, numbness, drowsiness, headaches, vomiting, sunken eyes or a sallow complexion may indicate a drug abuse problem in a person.

*symptoms of drug abuse*

An employee simply may be sick with an ailment that is not drug-related . . . or such physical symptoms could point to a drug abuse problem which needs to be addressed. For example, the nasal "infection" in fact may be bleeding caused by the "snorting" of cocaine.

(4) **Sudden Personality Changes**

Other signs that may indicate drug abuse in an employee are sudden and erratic mood or personality shifts. An employee who becomes excessively giddy, aggressive, or depressed, or inexplicably loses appetite or memory may be an employee on drugs.

In each situation, there are other explanations for these symptoms and behavior changes, and an employer should be careful not to jump to conclusions. Nonetheless, given the potential liabilities for failing to provide a safe workplace, the economic consequences of tolerating worker drug abuse, and business' responsibility to its workers and the community to address the drug abuse epidemic, employers cannot ignore the possibilities such evidence of drug abuse suggests.

*personality changes*

Beyond recognizing the symptoms of drug abuse in the **individual** employee, the employer also should analyze personnel and productivity records **overall.** Abnormal increases in absenteeism, accidents, compensation claims, and turnover, or abnormal decreases in production are further indications that a workplace drug abuse problem may exist.

Employers cannot afford to ignore a drug abuse problem on the job. To do so will only escalate the severity of the problem.

# Chapter 11

# The Value of Employee Assistance Programs

Employee assistance programs (EAPs) that address drug and alcohol abuse problems are becoming more common in the workplace.

Why? Because EAPs are effective and humane. They benefit employers, employees, and employees' families. The successful resolution of personal problems, such as drug and alcohol abuse, not only improves job performance, it preserves and enhances family life.

*why have EAPs?*

EAPs originally were developed to address employees suffering from alcoholism. In today's complex and fast-paced society, the range and frequency of personal and family problems have grown. EAPs have had corresponding growth in the scope of problems they address and their prevalence in employee benefit packages. EAPs often address not only drug and alcohol abuse, but also mental health, compulsive gambling, marital, financial, and family legal problems.

EAPs generally serve as an adjunct to a company's health care plan. They can include counseling, detoxification, and family support and re-enforcement. Often the costs of the rehabilitation program and an employee's time off the job are included in medical and disability coverage.

The ultimate goal of EAPs is rehabilitation . . . just as the ultimate goal of company drug abuse prevention programs —

along with deterrence — is and should be rehabilitation.

Why give an employee with a drug abuse problem a "second chance"? It is a smart business practice.

EAPs are good for morale — even the morale of those employees for whom the likelihood of drug or alcohol problems is truly remote. They demonstrate employers' responsiveness to, and caring for, their workers.

More important, EAPs often are effective **and** cost-effective. They are effective in helping some workers become drug-free, which, in turn, can be cost-effective for the employer because employee "down time" is reduced, health care costs are controlled, and highly trained employees are retained. Employers often have a sizeable investment in each of their employees, particularly for those individuals in positions requiring highly skilled workers. The training, experience, and integration into the company often are assets worth fighting to keep.

*cost effectiveness*

For example, in 1984 a program jointly administered by AT&T and the Communication Workers of America cost the company $1.3 million, but saved the company $3.3 million. Furthermore, the job retention for employees using the EAP was 97 percent.

Confidentiality is important. Protecting the privacy of employees involved in a drug rehabilitation program increases cooperation substantially. Also, the voluntary nature of such programs helps identify — and correct — many employee drug problems that employers would not have detected by themselves. In so doing, it

*confidentiality*

augments and enhances employers' efforts to prevent drug abuse among their employees.

# Chapter 12

# Guide to Dangerous Drugs

Education is critical to the prevention of drug abuse.

Drug abusers need to know why they should stop illegally using drugs and where they can get help. Just as important, non-users need to know how harmful drugs can be so that they never start.

Parents, teachers, employers, and co-workers should be able to identify a drug abuse problem, and should know how to help someone who has one.

*knowledge of drugs and their effects*

We all have to be aware of the effects of drugs on the mind and body — and the dangers associated with drug use. The choice is to be aware, or to be painfully unaware. The consequences of ignorance can be tragic.

Step one is to **know the drugs,** what they look like, how they are used, what they are called, and, most important, how they endanger the user.

The more information we know, the more people **who** know . . . the less of a threat drug abuse will be to our society. Prevention of drug abuse saves careers, families, even lives.

Recognizing that education about drugs is critical to drug abuse prevention, the following overview of dangerous drugs is provided, summarizing the drugs most commonly abused and most likely to affect workers.

## COCAINE

| | |
|---|---|
| **TYPE OF DRUG** | • Stimulant |
| | • Derived from leaves of coca plant grown in semitropical climate |
| **STREET NAMES** | • Coke, blow, snow, nose candy |
| **APPEARANCE** | • White crystalline powder |
| **HOW TAKEN** | • Inhaled through a tube into the nose |
| | • Smoked as a mixture ("freebasing") |
| | • Injected into the veins |
| **OTHER FORMS** | • Crack ("rock") — a solid, extremely addictive, and far more potent form of cocaine that is smoked and comes in light brown pellets or crystalline rocks |
| **EFFECTS** | • Produces brief but intense feelings of euphoria and competence |
| | • Stimulates central nervous system |
| | • Increases pulse, blood pressure, body temperature, and respiratory rate |
| | • Dilates eyes |
| **DANGERS** | • Psychological and physical dependency |
| | • Death caused by heart or respiratory failure |
| | • Bleeding and other damage to nasal passages |

- Injury or death caused by fire or explosion when "freebasing" because of use of flame with volatile solvents

- Paranoid psychosis, hallucinations, and other mental abnormalities

**COMMENTS**

Cocaine today is more potent, more abused, and more lethal than ever before in the United States.

There have been dramatic increases in cocaine-related deaths and medical emergencies in recent years.

Cocaine distribution is a multibillion dollar illegal operation that starts with 20 tons of cocaine being imported into the United States each year — usually from Bolivia or Peru — and ends with as much as 160 tons being sold illegally, once it has been mixed with sugar or other "cutting" agents, for as much as $2,500 an ounce.

Six million Americans use cocaine on a regular basis; there has been explosive growth in use in recent years.

**WORKPLACE IMPACT**

- **Major impact** on business community because of widespread insidious use by employees. Cocaine is the most dangerous commonly used illegal drug in the United States.

| | |
|---|---|
| **TYPE OF DRUG** | • Stimulant |
| | • Derived from the hemp plant Cannabis Sativa |
| **STREET NAMES** | • Pot, dope, grass, weed, reefer |
| **APPEARANCE** | • Greenish-brown dried and chopped leaves, small stems, and seeds |
| **HOW TAKEN** | • Smoked in hand-rolled cigarettes ("joints"), pipes, or water pipes ("bongs") |
| **OTHER FORMS** | • **THC** (tetrahydrocannabinol) — a stronger distilled form of the most active chemical substance in marijuana; comes in soft gelatin capsules that are swallowed |
| | • **Hashish** ("hash") — a refined form of marijuana that is more potent, is smoked in smaller doses, and comes in brown or black "cakes" or balls |
| **EFFECTS** | • Euphoric feeling akin to being mildly drunk |
| | • Increased heart rate |
| | • Bloodshot eyes |
| | • Dry mouth and throat |
| | • Increased appetite |
| | • Impaired coordination, concentration, and memory |
| **DANGERS** | The effects of marijuana use vary based on the personality and health of the user; the amount, frequency, and circumstances of use; and the |

potency of the drug. There are some common negative physical and mental effects, however, and medical research is uncovering more. Particularly for chronic users, these dangers **may** include:

- Deteriorating performance at work or at school

- "Burn out" involving lethargy, muddled thinking, acute frustration, depression, and self-absorption

- Decreased blood supply to the heart, which threatens the health of those with heart conditions

- Impaired sexual development and fertility, including production of abnormal sperm and menstrual irregularities

- Medical complications for pregnant women and developmental problems for offspring

- Damage to the lungs and pulmonary system

- Impulsive outbursts of anger, crying, or laughter

- Hallucinations caused by high doses

- Brain damage caused by long-term, continuous use

- Increased risk to safety and health as a result of impaired judgment and motor abilities — for example, increased likelihood of accidents while driving

**COMMENTS**

Marijuana is much more potent today than 10 years ago due to 5–7 times higher presence of THC, the drug's primary psychoactive ingredient.

Illegal sale of marijuana is a multibillion dollar industry in the United States. In fact, even user "accessories" are a multimillion dollar industry. Advocates of marijuana use and decriminalization have implemented sophisticated publishing and lobbying strategies.

Although some marijuana of a weaker strain is grown in the United States, most is imported illegally from Mexico, Columbia, and the Caribbean.

23 million Americans use marijuana on a regular basis, although there are some indications use is tapering off slightly.

**WORKPLACE IMPACT**

• **Major impact** on employers because use of marijuana is so common. Next to alcohol, marijuana is the most widely abused drug in the United States.

| | |
|---|---|
| **TYPE OF DRUG** | • Stimulant |
| | • Chemically manufactured |
| **STREET NAMES** | • Speed, uppers, ups, pep pills |
| **APPEARANCE** | • Capsules, pills, or tablets |
| **HOW TAKEN** | • Swallowed |
| | • Injected into the veins |
| | • Inhaled through a tube into the nose |
| **OTHER FORMS** | • **Methamphetamines** ("methedrine," "crank," "crystal") — a stimulant that, although not an amphetamine, has similar effects on the central nervous system, comes in several forms (white powder, pill, or off-white "rock"), and can be swallowed, injected or inhaled |
| **EFFECTS** | • Stimulates the central nervous system to produce feelings of increased alertness and activity and enhanced sense of well-being |
| | • Increases blood pressure and respiratory rate |
| | • Dilates pupils |
| | • Decreases appetite |
| | • Creates ability in some people to go without sleep for relatively long periods of time |
| **DANGERS** | • Side effects include dizziness, headaches, blurred vision, and sweating |

- Loss of coordination, tremors, and physical collapse caused by high doses
- Injections can cause sudden blood pressure increases resulting in fever, stroke, or heart failure
- Hallucinations, acute anxiety, paranoia, and other psychotic behavior possible
- Nervousness, irritability, and impulsive mood shifts are common
- "Crash" that occurs after amphetamines wear off can be traumatic and lead to suicidal behavior
- Overdoses can be fatal

**COMMENTS**

Stimulants are often legally manufactured but illegally distributed through diverse and extensive criminal activity.

"Speed" can cause some abusers to go without sleep as long as six days, followed by a "crash" marked by physical exhaustion and depression.

Caffeine found in coffee and cola is a very mild — and legal — stimulant.

Amphetamine-induced psychosis — caused by larger doses of the drug — often results in violent or self-destructive behavior due to the drug abuser's false sense of indestructability.

**WORKPLACE IMPACT**

**Major impact** on employers because of widespread use and availability of "uppers" . . . problem is exacerbated by misuse of prescription drugs. Some workers, believing such stimulants will increase productivity and creativity, ignore physical and mental dangers and, in fact, may believe their use of stimulants benefits their employers.

# BARBITURATES

| | |
|---|---|
| **TYPE OF DRUG** | • Depressant |
| | • Also known as sedatives |
| | • Chemically manufactured |
| **STREET NAMES** | • Downers, barbs, yellow jackets, red devils, blue devils |
| **APPEARANCE** | • Red, yellow, blue, or red and blue capsules |
| **HOW TAKEN** | • Swallowed |
| **OTHER FORMS** | • **Methaqualone** ("quaaludes," "ludes," or "sopors") — another form of sedatives, comes in tablet form, and is taken orally |
| | • **Tranquilizers** (including valium) — also are sedatives that depress the central nervous system, come in tablet or capsule form, and are taken orally |
| **EFFECTS** | • Effects of barbiturates — and other depressants — are similar to the effects of alcohol: calmness and relaxed muscles in small doses; slurred speech, impaired judgment, and loss of balance and coordination in larger doses |
| | • Effective as a medical treatment to relieve tension and calm nerves |
| **DANGERS** | • Heightened tension, restlessness, and insomnia when not "high" |
| | • Highly addictive, with intense withdrawal problems ranging from anxiety to convulsions to death |
| | • Overdoses result in respiratory depression, coma, and death |

- Especially dangerous for pregnant women because of possible birth defects and behavioral problems or chemical dependency in offspring

- Also especially dangerous when used in combination with alcohol because the risks of one multiply the risks of the other — often resulting in death

- Drowsiness and impaired motor abilities also result in higher accident rates

**COMMENTS**

While barbiturates and "ludes" are considered more dangerous than tranquilizers, all can result in serious illness or death.

Misuse of prescription drugs is especially common with depressants. Half of all sedative-related health emergencies result from nonmedical use of the drug by a person with a legitimate prescription.

**WORKPLACE IMPACT**

- **Major impact** on employers because of widespread hard-to-detect use . . . especially popular with employees in stressful and competitive jobs . . . users sometimes fail to recognize drug abuse because of "prescription" label . . . 10 million Americans now use prescription drugs, especially barbiturates and amphetamines, without an appropriate prescription. As with other drugs, barbiturates are a drug abuse problem for executives as well as rank-and-file employees.

Cocaine, marijuana, amphetamines, and barbiturates all have a major impact on the workplace. Along with alcohol, they represent the most common and most costly drug abuse problems for employers and employees.

But there are other drugs that, although less common, can be just as dangerous. These drugs — narcotics, hallucinogens, inhalants, and the analogs known as "designer drugs" — are as destructive to people on the job and in the home as the more commonly known and used drugs.

In truth, **all** drug abuse problems are major problems, and all need to be addressed by employers in a comprehensive, effective, and fair manner.

The "other" dangerous drugs include:

(1) **Narcotics** — Highly addictive and debilitating, narcotics are extremely dangerous drugs that affect the central nervous system. Medically used in small doses as painkillers, narcotics cause an initial feeling of euphoria, followed by drowsiness, nausea, and vomiting. Overdoses result in comas and death.

Narcotics include heroin, methadone, codeine, morphine, and such common painkillers as demerol and darvon. Most are derived from opium.

Needles used for injecting heroin and other narcotics can transmit AIDS, hepatitis, and other diseases.

Ninety percent of the narcotic abuse in the United States today involves heroin. Its most common form

*heroin*

is a white powder which first is heated and dissolved, and then is injected into the veins. Also known as "smack" and "horse," heroin can be sniffed or smoked. Although heroin use has not increased significantly in recent years, there are an estimated 500,000 heroin addicts in the U.S. These heroin addicts are unlikely to be employed in large numbers.

(2) **Hallucinogens** — Phencyclidine (PCP), lysergic acid diethylamide (LSD), and mescaline are the most common hallucinogens — drugs that distort perception of time and distance and can create illusions and hallucinations. Most are taken orally, although PCP commonly is smoked, sometimes when mixed with marijuana. All hallucinogens have an effect or "high" of a relatively long duration — eight hours or more. No hallucinogen has a medical use. Dependency is, perhaps, less likely for hallucinogens than any other commonly abused drug.

*PCP*

PCP is the most abused hallucinogen. An animal tranquilizer, PCP is notorious for causing bizarre, violent, and self-destructive behavior in humans. Also known as "angel dust" and "killer weed," PCP can create the same effects in a person as acute mental illness.

*LSD*

LSD, a less common hallucinogen known as "acid," has similar effects. It comes in liquid form, and most often is swallowed after having been placed on a sugar cube or blotting paper. The use of LSD sometimes results in bad "trips" or psychological reactions including exaggerated suspicions, fear, confusion, anxiety, loss of control, and subsequent flashbacks.

(3) **Inhalants** — Readily available in most households, inexpensive, and hard to control, inhalants are volatile substances that are abused by sniffing or inhaling. They include gasoline, airplane glue, paint thinner, aerosol propellants, and other common products that one seldom thinks of as drugs. Their abuse is particularly common among young school-aged people, and uncommon among adult employees.

*inhalants*

Inhalants, however, **are** extremely dangerous. They can cause anoxia (loss of oxygen), and can damage the brain, heart, kidneys, and digestive system. The sniffing or inhaling of inhalants also can be fatal.

(4) **Designer Drugs** — Underground chemists/pushers have modified the molecular structures of some illegal drugs to produce analogs known as "designer drugs." A relatively new phenomena, these analogs are unpredictable in their effects and often hundreds of times stronger than the drug they are intended to imitate. The heightened potency and unpredictability increase the likelihood of unintended but extremely harmful or lethal overdoses.

*drug analogs*

The most common street names are "synthetic heroin," "China white," and "ecstasy." There currently are available analogs of narcotics, amphetamines, and PCP.

In most cases, prevention of their sale is beyond the reach of the law.

Because of their new molecular structures, these drugs usually are not yet classified as illegal drugs by federal and state food and drug administration officials. The result is extremely dangerous and unknown drugs being sold "over the counter" as easily — and legally — as chewing gum.

*"ecstasy"*

Medical science also has not caught up with these analogs. However, many scientists now believe "ecstasy," which is especially popular with college students, causes brain damage.

In conclusion, there is no "safe" drug abuse. Those who abuse drugs — any drug — are gambling with their lives. Drugs, which so often can perform medical miracles, also can be deadly poison.

# Chapter 13

# Alcohol Abuse: An Even Bigger Workplace Problem

Alcohol is the most commonly abused drug in America . . . and in American workplaces.

The drug abuse issue has captured the attention of the public, media, government, and business community in recent years. But our country cannot afford to address one problem — drug abuse — while overlooking what continues to be an even bigger problem — alcohol abuse.

*extent of the alcohol problem*

Twelve million Americans are alcoholics. Another ninety million are "social drinkers" who have had alcohol at least once in the last month. All of the alcoholics have a major problem; some of the social drinkers do.

Alcohol does not pose a danger to most people who drink it. Alcohol is a common and established part of American culture — in the workplace alone it is an integral part of most Christmas parties, company picnics, and social receptions. In most cases, its use is legal, safe, and accepted.

Nonetheless, alcohol abuse is a national tragedy. While the drug abuse epidemic has grown substantially in recent years, alcohol abuse remains a far more common and costly problem.

An estimated half of all alcohol problems occur among "social" drinkers. These problems include alcohol-related vehicle accidents, which have claimed as many as 25,000 lives a year in the United States.

The effects of alcohol abuse on the workplace include:

(1) **Increased absenteeism** — The Employee Assistance Society of North America (EASNA) found that absenteeism among problem drinkers ranges from 3.8 to 8.3 times greater than normal. Perhaps even more significant — but less obvious — is the fact that a non-alcoholic member of an alcoholic's family uses 10 times as much sick leave as normal.

(2) **Reduced productivity** — The Research Triangle Institute estimated that alcohol abuse cost employers $65 billion in productivity losses in 1983, nearly double the $33 billion cost of decreased productivity caused by abuse of all other drugs. Beyond reduction in the **amount** of work being performed, there also are substantial reductions in the **quality** of work being performed. Reduced quality — like reduced productivity — hurts both consumers and American competitiveness versus foreign producers.

*effects on the workplace*

(3) **Increased accident rates** — EASNA also found that up to 40 percent of industrial fatalities and 47 percent of industrial injuries are related to alcohol abuse and alcoholism. Workplace accident rates are two-to-three times higher for alcoholics than normal.

(4) **Increased health care costs** — Alcohol abuse also costs billions of dollars in increased health care costs, much of which is borne by the business community. The National Institute

on Alcoholism and Alcohol Abuse (NIAAA) reports that the average monthly health care costs for a family with an alcoholic member are $207 per person, while the average costs for families with no alcoholic members are $107 per person. An alcoholic's average health care costs increase from $150 a month two years before treatment to $450 a month six months before treatment to $1,370 in the final month before treatment.

Overall, alcohol abuse costs employers $117 billion a year, up 30 percent in only three years. Like the abuse of other drugs, however, while the economic costs of alcohol abuse are enormous, the human costs are even larger.

*alcohol dependency*

The National Institute of Mental Health reports that 13.6 percent of all adults have experienced clinically significant alcohol addiction or abuse at some point in their lives — making alcohol dependence the most common form of mental disorder in America.

More than four times as many people regularly use alcohol as regularly use marijuana. While 7 to 8 percent of all employees abuse alcohol, "only" 2 to 3 percent are adversely affected by marijuana. Furthermore, the NIAAA reports that half of all "problem drinkers" are working.

The bottom line on alcohol abuse: the life span of a heavy drinker is shortened 12 years on average.

Employers need to address alcohol abuse in the workplace with the same commitment that they address the abuse of other drugs. Identification of a drug or alcohol problem, enforcement of company policy, and rehabilitation of the employee should

be pursued in an equally fair and comprehensive manner. To address one problem and ignore the other is not only unfair,
it is senseless.

Alcohol abuse **is** a major drug problem
in the workplace. Therefore, the following
profile of alcohol and its effects is provided, consistent with the summaries of
drugs included in the section entitled
"Guide to Dangerous Drugs."

## ALCOHOL

| | |
|---|---|
| **TYPE OF DRUG** | • Sedative-anesthetic |
| | • Alcohol **is a drug** that, like sedatives, depresses the central nervous system |
| | • Produced by fermenting process involving natural ingredients (sugar and yeast spores) |
| **STREET NAMES** | • Liquor, cocktails, spirits, booze |
| **APPEARANCE** | • Ethyl alcohol, the psychoactive ingredient in beer, wine, and distilled liquor, is a colorless liquid with a strong, distinctive smell |
| **HOW TAKEN** | • Beer, which is less than ten percent alcohol in content, is drunk |
| | • Wine, which also is less than ten percent alcohol, is drunk, sometimes in combination with non-alcoholic drinks |
| | • Distilled liquor, with an alcohol content usually more than 40 percent, also is drunk, and often is mixed with soft drinks, fruit juices, or water |

- Some recipes include alcohol as a ingredient in food

**OTHER FORMS**
- Besides its use for drinking and cooking, other forms of alcohol are used as ingredients in medicine, solvents, preservatives, and cleaning agents, and for a wide range of other purposes

**EFFECTS**
- Appears initially to act as a stimulant, invigorating thought and activity

- Produces feelings of relaxation, reduced anxiety, and mild euphoria

- Induces, as consumption increases, progressive stages of sedation, anesthesia, and, in very large quantities, coma

- Causes intoxication, dependence, and tolerance

- Causes reddening of the whites of the eyes

- Reduces rapid eye movement (visual range, perception, and reactions)

- Induces sleep

- Impedes the function of the portions of the brain that affect self-control

- Impedes memory by disrupting transfer of recent memory to long-term storage banks

**DANGERS**
Alcohol has different effects on people depending on a wide range of physical, mental, and environmental circumstances. For most people, alcohol acts as a

sedative. The common — and often dangerous — physical and mental responses to alcohol abuse are:

- Physical and psychological dependency

- Impaired coordination, responses, attention, tracking, and judgment

- Drowsiness or loss of consciousness

- Fatal respiratory or heart failure caused by large quantities being consumed in a short time period

- Toxic or inflamatory damage to the liver, heart, pancreas, and gastrointestinal tract **caused** by excessive and continuous consumption; severe damage to the brain and nervous system **may be caused** by excessive and continuous consumption

- Increased susceptibility to disease

- Malnutrition

- Cancer of the mouth, larynx, esophagus, and liver

- Increased likelihood of injury or death resulting from accidents in motor vehicles, on the job, and at home due to detrimental effect on driving and other skilled tasks

- Distinct withdrawal syndrome, including delirium tremens, the stages of which are progressively traumatic and painful, and even fatal

- Especially dangerous when used in combination with other drugs, especially barbiturates

- Especially dangerous for pregnant women because of spontaneous abortions, birth defects, or physical and mental retardation (also known as fetal alcohol syndrome)

**COMMENTS**

Alcohol plays an important cultural and social role in our society. Used in moderation, its use can be safe and appropriate. Alcohol **use** is not necessarily the problem; alcohol **abuse** is. Used in excess, alcohol can and does destroy lives.

Twelve million Americans have the disease of alcoholism. Nearly 150 million Americans drink alcohol at least occasionally, including more than two-thirds of all adults in the United States.

Since 1980, alcohol use in the United States has declined 4 percent, but alcoholism has increased 8 percent.

**WORKPLACE IMPACT**

- **Major Impact** on employers because alcohol abuse is so common and so socially accepted . . . the fine line that exists between social drinkers and problem drinkers may obscure the extent of the alcohol abuse problem. Seven to 8 percent of the work force abuses alcohol. Alcohol abuse costs employers $117 billion, nearly twice as much as the $60 billion annual cost to employers of abuse of other drugs.

# WHAT IS ALCOHOLISM?

Alcoholism is a disease marked by continued excessive or compulsive use of alcoholic drinks.

An alcoholic is a person who loses the ability to determine how much alcohol is "too much." If a person lacks the self-control not to drink or to stop drinking, that person is dependent on alcohol.

The warning signs of alcoholism include: a steady increase in drinking, frequent drinking binges, the need to drink to face certain situations, drinking alone, and early morning drinking.

Alcoholism is potentially fatal.

# Chapter 14

# Some Additional Legal Requirements And Concerns

Some employers are subject to special requirements imposed by the federal government regarding job applicants or employees who are former or current drug or alcohol abusers.

*application*

These requirements **only** apply to: (1) federal contractors or subcontractors receiving $2,500 or more in federal contracts, and (2) all employers who receive federal financial assistance such as research grants or Small Business Administration loans.

*handicap discrimination*

**The Federal Rehabilitation Act of 1973,** 29 U.S.C. §793 and 794 (more commonly referred to as §503 and 504) ("the Act") prohibits employers who receive federal funds from discriminating against handicapped persons. Although the Act includes prior drug abuse or alcoholism in its definition of "handicap," it was amended in 1978 specifically to exclude current usage if it impairs job performance.

Therefore, the Act not only provides legal rights for past drug or alcohol abusers, it also provides legal rights for **current** drug and alcohol abusers, unless their substance abuse detrimentally affects job performance or presents a danger to themselves or others.

If an employee, of an employer who receives federal funds, uses drugs or alcohol, that person cannot be subjected to employment discrimination if their use does not interfere with job performance or pose unreasonable risks to the property or safety of others.

**What is "employment discrimination?"** Employers are prohibited from refusing to hire, retain, or promote a person, or from discriminatorily applying terms and conditions of employment. For example, a federal contractor **cannot:**

- Refuse to hire a job applicant because he or she has a drug abuse history,

- Provide less insurance coverage or require higher employee co-payments for workers with a drug abuse history,

*what covered employers cannot do*

- **Ask** a job applicant if he or she has ever abused drugs or ever been treated for drug abuse (however, an employer **can** ask a job applicant if he or she has a disability which would impair job performance and **can** ask questions regarding **current** drug use),

- Use the results of job-related pre-employment medical examinations (including drug tests) to discriminate against qualified handicapped individuals, including former substance abusers, or

- Pass over for promotion, special training, or salary increase any employee: (1) because he or she has a drug abuse history, **or** (2) because he or she currently uses drugs (provided that the drug use does not affect job performance or endanger persons or property).

However, keep in mind that:

(1) The Federal Rehabilitation Act applies **only** to those employers receiving federal funds, not all employers,

(2) The Act does **not** require employers to hire all job applicants who are former substance abusers — or any one job applicant with such a history. It **only** requires that they be treated equally with other job applicants and evaluated based on their job qualifications,

(3) The Act does **not** require employers to hire or retain persons unable to perform their jobs, or persons violating bonafide company rules or policies which are non-discriminatory in application and for which violation would legally justify the firing of any other employee, and

(4) The Act does **not** require employers to hire or retain persons engaged in — or with a history of — criminal activity. For example, employers can inquire, under the Act, if a job applicant has any prior **convictions** for driving while intoxicated (DWI) or illegal possession of drugs. However, employers should **not** ask about prior **arrests** because such inquiries can lead to Title VII discrimination charges because of the disparate proportion of minority arrests in many jurisdictions and the inconclusive nature of arrests vis-a-vis convictions. An employer **does** have a right to deny employment to those persons who are convicted felons. For example, employers can deny employment to job applicants with DWI convictions because, in doing so, employers are "discriminating" against the applicants based on the fact that they are felons, not because they are handicapped.

*applicants with criminal records*

Because federal law considers a prior history of drug abuse a handicap, employers who discriminate against individuals in this protected class may face legal action in a number of forums.

Federal contractors and subcontractors may be subject to complaints filed under §503 with the Office of Federal Contract Compliance Programs (OFCCP) of the U.S. Department of Labor. Potential penalties include loss of existing contracts and contract debarment for future federal contracts.

*OFCCP penalties*

Employers receiving federal dollars through grants or loans may face complaints filed under §504 with the federal agency which provided the funds **or** may be subject to lawsuits filed in federal or state courts. Potential penalties include instatement or reinstatement, back-pay awards, and liability for attorneys' fees.

Furthermore, a number of states prohibit job discrimination based on handicaps or disabilities — statutes that explicitly or implicitly include persons with substance abuse histories within the definition of "handicapped." These statutes do not limit application to employers receiving public funds, but apply to all employers within the jurisdiction of the state.

*state and local laws*

Although such statutes now exist in only a few states, the law as a whole regarding drug abuse and drug testing in the workplace is changing constantly.

For example, the city of San Francisco prohibits random drug testing in the public and private sectors in almost all work situations (San Francisco Ordinance No. 527-85, 1985), and California **requires** private employers to permit their employees to voluntarily undergo alcohol rehabilitation, provided it does not impose undue hardship on the employer (the employer does have the right to refuse to hire or to discharge the person if his or her alcoholism is incapacitating). (Cal. Labor Section 1025–1028).

*the need for legal counsel*

Before implementing a drug abuse prevention program, drug testing, or substance abuse-related hiring policies, employers must do their homework, keep current with the law, and consult with legal counsel.

# Chapter 15

# How Drug Use Affects Us

Is drug use glamorous?

Some people think drugs increase your confidence, your energy, your fun. And they're right . . . for some people, some drugs have some of those effects . . . some of the time . . . in the short-run.

People who abuse drugs believe that by smoking, snorting, popping or shooting, a person can be more sophisticated and popular. Each of these methods of drug use also can change people in other ways. They can become addicted or violently ill. Some even die.

*are drug users glamorous?*

Some people in the "fast lane" feel they "need" drugs to get up, stay up, keep up. Drugs are a status symbol — like a sports car or fancy clothes. Cocaine is called "the yuppie drug." Synthetically manufactured pills are called "designer drugs." A fashionable piece of gold jewelry can double as the means of carrying, cutting, or administering drugs.

Songs, movies, and clothing sometimes glorify drug use. Based on media reports, drug use **is** a part of the lifestyles of some sports and rock stars. But it also affects Americans in less glamorous jobs, such as welders and waitresses. Drugs are more available, more potent, and more accepted in the United States than ever before.

Every reliable study, however, has shown that drug use compromises the user's health and basic abilities. Some of the "glamorous" ways drug use can affect your **mind** are:

- giddiness
- aggressiveness
- depression
- indecisiveness
- lethargy
- false sense of security
- loss of appetite
- loss of memory
- impaired judgment
- impaired learning and retention
- impaired vision and depth perception
- chemical dependency
- withdrawal symptoms
- hallucinations
- violent mood shifts
- paranoia, schizophrenia, and other psychotic behavior

*drugs' effects on the mind*

More critically, some of the "glamorous" ways drug use can affect your **body** are:

- slurred speech
- impaired balance, dexterity, reflexes, and coordination
- chills
- sweating
- numbness
- headaches
- vomiting

- muscle deterioration
- sunken eyes
- sallow complexion
- liver ailments
- aching limbs
- skin infections
- blood diseases
- high blood pressure

- hemorrhaging
- constriction of coronary arteries
- convulsions
- loss of sensation
- loss of consciousness
- stroke
- permanent brain damage
- paralysis
- respiratory failure
- cardiac arrest

. . . and . . .

- death

The health effects listed above could be caused by factors other than drugs. But, given the widespread use and abuse of drugs in our country — 23 million Americans using marijuana on a regular basis, six million Americans using cocaine on a regular basis — they are **warning signs** and should be investigated if they persist.

Thousands of Americans die from drug overdoses each year — sports stars, rock stars, welders, and waitresses. Tens of thousands more are killing themselves more slowly by repeated drug use. Recent experiences have demonstrated that even a healthy person, without any history of illegal drug use, can be killed by abusing drugs such as "crack" a single time.

For the drug pushers, drug abuse is mass murder; for the drug users, drug abuse is suicide; and for society — our society — drug abuse is a national tragedy.

Drug use is not glamorous.

# Appendix A

# Other Reference Sources

## I. ARTICLES AND PUBLICATIONS

- "Alcohol & Drugs in the Workplace: Costs, Controls, and Controversies," a special report of the Bureau of National Affairs, 1986.

- "Alcohol . . . The Most Abused Drug in America," "Eight More Dangerous Drugs You Should Know About," "Cocaine. It's Not a Harmless Drug," and "The Dangers of Marijuana," Your Kids & Drugs, Spot It/Stop It pamphlet series, Peoples Drug Stores, 1986.

- "American Drugs," *U.S. News & World Report*, July 28, 1986.

- "Battling the Enemy Within," *Time*, March 17, 1986.

- "Business Must Lead the War on Drugs," *Coalition Report*, Clearinghouse on Business Coalitions for Health Action, September 1986.

- "Can You Pass the Job Test?," *Newsweek*, May 5, 1986.

- Chapman, Fern Schumer, "The Ruckus Over Medical Testing," *Fortune*, August 19, 1985.

- *Drug Abuse and the Workplace*, Associated Builders and Contractors, Inc., 1985.

- *Drug and Alcohol/Fitness for Duty, EEI Guide to Effective Policy Development*, Edison Electric Institute, August 1985.

- Fein, Rashi, *Alcohol in America: The Price We Pay*, CareInstitute, 1984.

- Hoffer, William, "A New Focus on Drugs," *Nation's Business*, December 1986.

- Hoffer, William, "Business' War on Drugs," *Nation's Business*, September 1986.

- Krizay, John and Edward J Carels, *The Fifty Billion Dollar Drain: Alcohol, Drugs and the High Cost of Insurance*, CareInstitute, 1986.

- "Marijuana," "Marijuana and Alcohol Combinations," and "Cocaine: Some Questions and Answers," pamphlet series, the American Council for Drug Education, 1983.

- Marcus, Ruth and Margaret Engel, "Many Employers Testing Workers for Drug Use," *Washington Post*, February 2, 1986.

- Serrin, William, "Drug Tests Promote Safety, Many Say," *New York Times*, September 16, 1986.

- Shepard, Ira Michael and Harry Olsen, "Employee Privacy Rights, A Management Guide," College and University Personnel Association, 1986.

- Susser, Peter A., and Denis R. Zegar, *The NAWGA Model Substance Abuse Program*, National Wholesale Grocers' Association, 1986.

- Thompson, Barlow H., Jr., "UNOCAL Gets Tough on Drugs in the Workplace," *Coalition Report*, Clearinghouse on Business Coalitions for Health Action, January 1986.

- "Urine Drug Testing — A Hot Issue," *MBG Newsletter*, MBG Management Services, Inc., 1986.

- Waldholz, Michael, "Drug Testing in the Workplace: Whose Rights Take Precedence?," *Wall Street Journal*, November 11, 1986.

## II. U.S. GOVERNMENT PUBLICATIONS

- *Controlled Substances: Use, Abuse and Effects, Drug Enforcement Administration*, U.S. Department of Justice, 1985.

- *Interdisciplinary Approaches to the Problem of Drug Abuse in the Workplace*, Consensus Summary, National Institute on Drug Abuse (NIDA), U.S. Department of Health and Human Services (HHS), 1986.

- "Marijuana," "Stimulants and Cocaine," "Inhalants," and "Sedative-Hypnotics," *Just Say No* pamphlet series, NIDA, HHS, 1984.

- *Urine Testing for Drugs of Abuse*, Research Monograph Series 73, NIDA, HHS, 1986.

- Walsh, J. Michael and Richard L. Hawks, "Employee Drug Screening Q & A," NIDA, HHS, 1986.

- *What Works, Schools Without Drugs*, U.S. Department of Education, 1986.

## III. OTHER SOURCES OF INFORMATION

- ACTION Drug Prevention Program, 806 Connecticut Avenue, N.W., Washington, D.C. 20525. 1-800-241-9746.

- American Council for Drug Education, 6193 Executive Boulevard, Rockville, Maryland 20852. (301) 984-5700.

- Drug Enforcement Administration, U.S. Department of Justice, Washington, D.C. 20537. (202) 633-1000.

- Narcotics Anonymous, P.O. Box 9999, Van Nuys, California 91409. (818) 780-3951.

- National Clearinghouse for Alcohol Information, P.O. Box 2345, Rockville, Maryland 20852. (301) 468-2600.

- National Clearinghouse for Drug Abuse Information, P.O. Box 416, Kensington, Maryland 20795. (301) 443-6500.

- National Federation of Parents for Drug Free Youth, 1820 Franwall Avenue, Suite 16, Silver Spring, Maryland 20902. 1-800-554-KIDS.

- National Institute on Drug Abuse, 5600 Fishers Lane, Rockville, Maryland 20850. 1-800-638-2045.

- PRIDE (Parents' Resource Institute for Drug Education), 100 Edgewood Avenue, Suite 1002, Atlanta, GA 30303. (404) 658- 2548.

# Appendix B

# Tollfree Telephone Numbers for Drug Abuse Counseling and Assistance

- ACTION/PRIDE DRUG
  INFORMATION LINE................. 1-800-241-9746
- ALCOHOL HOTLINE .............. 1-800-ALCOHOL
- COCAINE HELPLINE ............. 1-800-COCAINE
- NATIONAL FEDERATION
  OF PARENTS FOR
  DRUG-FREE YOUTH ................1-800-554-KIDS
- NATIONAL INSTITUTE ON
  DRUG ABUSE, HHS ................. 1-800-638-2045
- NIDA COCAINE HOTLINE........... 1-800-662-HELP
- NIDA WORKPLACE HELPLINE ....... 1-800-843-4971

# Appendix C
# State Agencies Dealing With Drug Abuse

ALABAMA
Department of Mental Health and Mental Retardation
Substance Abuse Prevention Section
P.O. Box 3700
Montgomery, Alabama 36193-5001
(205) 271-9250

ALASKA
State Office of Alcoholism and Drug Abuse (SOADA)
P.O. Box H-05F
Juneau, Alaska 99811-0607
(907) 586-6201

ARIZONA
Office of Community Behavioral Health
Department of Health Services
701 East Jefferson, Suite 400A
Phoenix, Arizona 85034
(602) 255-1152

ARKANSAS
Office of Alcohol and Drug Abuse Prevention
Department of Human Services
1515 West 7th, Suite 310
Little Rock, Arkansas 72201
(501) 371-2603

CALIFORNIA
Department of Alcohol and Drug Programs
111 Capitol Mall
Sacramento, California 95814
(916) 322-6690 — drug abuse
(916) 323-2087 — alcohol abuse

COLORADO
Milehigh Counsel on Alcoholism and Drug Abuse
1776 South Jackson, Suite 615
Denver, Colorado 80210
(303) 759-5555

CONNECTICUT
Alcohol and Drug Abuse Commission
999 Asylum Avenue
Hartford, Connecticut 06105
(203) 566-7458

DELAWARE
Delaware Bureau of Alcoholism and Drug Abuse
1901 North Dupont Highway
New Castle, Delaware 19720
(302) 421-6101

DISTRICT OF COLUMBIA
Office of Health Planning and Development
425 Eye Street, N.W., Suite 3210
Washington, D.C. 20001
(202) 724-5637

FLORIDA
Alcohol, Drug Abuse and Mental Health Program
1370 Winewood Boulevard
Building 6 — Room 156
Tallahassee, Florida 32399-0700
(904) 488-0900

GEORGIA
Alcohol and Drug Abuse Services
Division of Mental Health
878 Peachtree Street, N.E., Room 319
Atlanta, Georgia 30309
(404) 894-4204

HAWAII
Alcohol and Drug Abuse Branch
Department of Health
P.O. Box 3378
Honolulu, Hawaii 96801
(808) 548-4280

IDAHO
Bureau of Substance Abuse
Department of Health and Welfare
450 West State Street
Boise, Idaho 83702
(208) 334-5935 or (208) 334-5700

ILLINOIS
Department of Alcoholism and Substance Abuse
100 West Randolph Street, Suite 5-600
Chicago, Illinois 60601
(312) 917-3840

INDIANA
Division of Addiction Services
Department of Mental Health
117 East Washington Street
Indianapolis, Indiana
(317) 232-7816

IOWA
Division of Substance Abuse
Lucas Building, 4th Floor
321 East 12th Street
Des Moines, Iowa 50319
(515) 281-3641

KANSAS
Alcohol and Drug Abuse Services
2700 West 6th Street
Topeka, Kansas 66606
(913) 296-3925

KENTUCKY
Cabinet for Human Resources
Division for Substance Abuse
275 East Main
Frankfort, Kentucky 70621
(502) 564-2880

LOUISIANA
Office of Prevention and Recovery From Alcohol and Drug
Abuse
P.O. Box 53129
Baton Rouge, Louisiana 70892
(504) 922-0725

MAINE
Office of Alcohol and Drug Abuse Prevention
235 State Street
Augusta, Maine 04333
(207) 289-2771

MARYLAND
Drug Abuse Administration
O'Connor Building — 4th floor
201 West Preston Street
Baltimore, Maryland 21201
(301) 225-6910

MASSACHUSETTS
Division of Alcoholism & Drug Rehabilitation
150 Tremont Street, 6th floor
Boston, Massachusetts 02111
(617) 727-1960

MICHIGAN
Office of Substance Abuse Services
3423 North Logan Street
P.O. Box 30035
Lansing, Michigan 30035
(517) 335-8809

MINNESOTA
Chemical Dependency Program Division
Department of Human Services
The Space Center Building
444 Lafayette Road
St. Paul, Minnesota 55155
prevention programs: (612) 296-8574;
treatment (612) 296-4611

MISSISSIPPI
Department of Mental Health
Division of Alcohol and Drug Abuse
1500 Woolfolk Bldg.
Jackson, Mississippi 39201
(601) 359-1297

MISSOURI
Division of Alcohol and Drug Abuse
1915 Southridge Drive
P.O. Box 687
Jefferson City, Missouri 65102
(314) 751-4942

MONTANA
Alcohol-Drug Abuse Division,
Department of Institutions
1539 11th Avenue
Helena, Montana 59620
(406) 444-2827

NEBRASKA
Division of Alcoholism and Drug Abuse
Department of Public Institutions
P.O. Box 94728
Lincoln, Nebraska 68509-4728
(402) 471-2851

NEVADA
Bureau of Alcohol and Drug Abuse, Human Resources/
Rehabilitations
505 East King Street, Room 500
Carson City, Nevada 89710
(702) 885-4790

NEW HAMPSHIRE
Office of Alcohol and Drug Abuse Prevention
6 Hazen Drive
Concord, New Hampshire 03301
(603) 271-4638

NEW JERSEY
Division of Alcoholism
129 East Hanover Street, CN362
Trenton, New Jersey 08625-0362
(609) 292-0729
Drug treatment: (609) 292-0728

NEW MEXICO
Drug Abuse Bureau
Health and Environment Department
P.O. Box 968
Santa Fe, New Mexico 87504
(505) 827-2589 or (505) 827-2597

NEW YORK
Division of Alcoholism and Alcohol Abuse
194 Washington Avenue
Albany, New York 12210
(800) ALCALLS (New York only)
(518) 474-3377 (all other states)

NORTH CAROLINA
Division of Mental Health and Mental Retardation
Alcohol and Drug Abuse Section
325 North Salisbury Street
Raleigh, North Carolina 27611
(919) 733-4670

NORTH DAKOTA
Department of Human Resources
Division of Alcoholism and Drug Abuse
State Capitol Building
Judicial Wing
Bismarck, North Dakota 58505
(701) 224-2769

OHIO
Bureau on Alcohol Abuse & Recovery
Department of Mental Health
170 North High Street, 3rd floor
Columbus, Ohio 43215
(614) 466-3445
Bureau of Drug Abuse
Columbus, Ohio (614) 466-7893

OKLAHOMA
Reach Out Hotline, Public Information and Prevention
Department of Mental Health
4545 North Lincoln Boulevard
P.O. Box 53277 — Capitol Station
Oklahoma City, Oklahoma 73152
(800) 522-9054 (Oklahoma only)
(405) 521-0044, x321 (all other states)

OREGON
Office of Alcohol and Drug Abuse Programs
301 Public Service Building
Salem, Oregon 97310
(503) 378-2163

PENNSYLVANIA
ENCORE, Office of Drug Abuse Programs
Health & Welfare Building, Room 929
Harrisburg, Pennsylvania 17120
(800) 932-0912 (Pennsylvania only)
(717) 787-9761 (all other states)

RHODE ISLAND
Department of Mental Health, Retardation & Hospitals
Division of Substance Abuse
Substance Abuse Administration Building
Cranston, Rhode Island 02920
(401) 464-2191

SOUTH CAROLINA
South Carolina Commission on Alcohol and Drug Abuse
3700 Forest Drive
Columbia, South Carolina 29204
(803) 734-9520

SOUTH DAKOTA
Division of Alcohol and Drug Abuse
523 East Capitol
Pierre, South Dakota 57501
(605) 773-3123

TENNESSEE
Division of Alcohol and Drug Abuse
Department of Mental Health
505 Deadrick Street
Nashville, Tennessee 37219
prevention: (615) 741-4241
treatment: (615) 741-1924

TEXAS
Commission on Alcoholism and Drug Abuse Prevention
1705 Guadalupe Street
Austin, Texas 78701
(512) 463-5510

UTAH
Division of Alcoholism and Drugs
150 West North Temple, 4th floor
Salt Lake City, Utah 84103
(801) 533-6532

VERMONT
Alcohol and Drug Abuse Division
103 South Main Street — 1 North
Waterbury, Vermont 05676
(802) 241-2170

VIRGINIA
Prevention Information Services
Department of Mental Health & Retardation
P.O. Box 1797
Richmond, Virginia 23214
(804) 786-1530

WASHINGTON
Bureau of Alcohol and Substance Abuse
Mail Stop OB44W
Olympia, Washington, 98504
(206) 753-5866

WEST VIRGINIA
Division of Alcoholism and Drug Abuse
Department of Health
1024 First Avenue
Montgomery, West Virginia 25136
(304) 348-2276

WISCONSIN
Office of Alcohol and Drug Abuse
Bureau of Community Programs
P.O. Box 7851
Madison, Wisconsin 53707
(608) 266-2717

WYOMING
Division of Community Programs
Department of Health and Social Services
3rd floor — Hathaway Building
Cheyenne, Wyoming 82002
(307) 777-6493

# Appendix D

# States Mandating Health Benefits for Employees with Drug or Alcohol Abuse Problems

In June 1985, the U.S. Supreme Court in *Metropolitan Life Insurance Company v. Massachusetts*, 85 L.Ed.2d 728 (1985) upheld a Massachusetts law that requires insurance companies to provide minimum health benefits coverage in their insurance policies. The decision permits states to require private insurance companies to include certain benefits in policies they believe are in the public interest.

At issue in the *Metropolitan* case was whether a Massachusetts law mandating minimum mental health benefit coverage in insurance policies was preempted by the Employee Retirement Income Security Act of 1974 (ERISA). Section 514 of ERISA is the "business of insurance" exception to ERISA preemption. The Court held that the state's mandated benefit statute fell within the "business of insurance" exception. Thus, the ERISA exemption for state health mandates was eliminated for private insurance company health policies. Self-funded programs remain exempt from these mandates.

The Health Insurance Association of America reports that, in 1986, 37 states mandated either coverage of, or the offer of coverage for, alcoholism treatment in insurance company policies. They are:

| | | |
|---|---|---|
| Alabama | Minnesota | Oregon |
| California | Mississippi | Pennsylvania |
| Colorado | Missouri | Rhode Island |
| Connecticut | Montana | South Dakota |
| Florida | Nebraska | Tennessee |
| Illinois | Nevada | Texas |
| Kansas | New Jersey | Utah |
| Kentucky | New Mexico | Vermont |
| Louisiana | New York | Virginia |
| Maine | North Carolina | Washington |
| Maryland | North Dakota | West Virginia |
| Massachusetts | Ohio | Wisconsin |
| Michigan | | |

In 1986, 17 states mandated either coverage of, or the offer of coverage for, drug abuse treatment in insurance company policies. They are:

| | | |
|---|---|---|
| Connecticut | Minnesota | Oregon |
| Kansas | Missouri | Tennessee |
| Louisiana | Montana | Texas |
| Maine | Nevada | Virginia |
| Maryland | North Carolina | Wisconsin |
| Michigan | North Dakota | |

# Appendix E

# Sample Company Policy And Authorizations

Following are three sample statements or authorizations for use by a company in its drug abuse prevention program:

(1) **Company Policy on Alcohol, Drugs, and Controlled Substances,**

(2) **Authorization for Testing,** and

(3) **Authorization for Release and Use of Testing Information.**

Copies of the company's policy statement should be distributed to all employees **and** all job applicants. Authorizations should be signed and dated: (1) by job applicants before their hire, and (2) by employees before drug testing.

The sample policy statement and authorization forms were provided by Nancy L. Abell and Paul W. Cane, Jr. of the law firm of Paul, Hastings, Janofsky and Walker in Los Angeles, California.

They stress — and the author reiterates — that these are only sample statements and authorizations and that actual company documents must be tailored: (1) for consistency with other company policies, and (2) for compliance with federal, state, and local requirements.

## COMPANY POLICY ON ALCOHOL, DRUGS, AND CONTROLLED SUBSTANCES

1. **Policy Objectives** — The Company has an obligation to its employees, customers, and the public at large to take reasonable steps to assure safety in the workplace, safety and quality in the products it sells, and safety in their distribution.

2. Prohibitions — To this end, the Company reaffirms its policy that the following are strictly **prohibited:**

(a) Reporting to work under the influence of intoxicants, drugs, or controlled substances.

(b) The use, possession, transfer, or trafficking of intoxicants, illegal drugs, or controlled substances in any amount or in any manner (i) on Company premises or in Company vehicles at any time, whether or not performing Company business, or (ii) while performing Company business anywhere, including off-Company property. Any employee convicted of a felony attributable to the use, possession, or sale of intoxicants, illegal drugs, or controlled substances on or off Company property will be subject to disciplinary action, including immediate termination.

(c) The use in any way of Company property or the employee's position within the Company to make or traffic intoxicants, illegal drugs, or controlled substances.

(d) Any other use, possession, or trafficking of intoxicants, illegal drugs, or controlled substances in a manner which is detrimental to the interest of the Company.

3. **Notice to Supervisor of Legal Drugs or Medications** — Any employee who is taking a drug or medication, whether or not prescribed by the employee's physician, which may adversely affect that employee's ability to perform work in a safe or productive manner is required to report such use of medication to his or her supervisor. This includes drugs which are known or advertised as possibly affecting judgment, coordination, or any of the senses, including those which may cause drowsiness or dizziness. The supervisor in conjunction with the Personnel Department then will determine whether the employee can remain at work and whether any work restrictions will be necessary.

4. **Company's Right To Search** — When the Company has any reason to believe that an employee is violating any aspect of this policy, he or she may be asked by the Com-

pany to submit immediately at any time (including breaks and the lunch period) to a search of his or her person and/or to make his or her locker, lunch box, briefcase, purse, pockets, wallet, personal belongings, desk, vehicles, or any other receptacle he or she uses or has access to, available for inspection. Entry on to Company premises constitutes consent to searches and inspections. Refusal to consent to a search or inspection when requested by the Company constitutes insubordination and a violation of company policy.

5. **Company's Right to Test** — The employee may be asked to submit to a medical examination and/or eye, blood, urine, or other medical tests.

6. **Disciplinary Action for Violation of the Policy** — Any employee who violates any aspect of this policy, including refusal to submit to any of the above-described searches, inspections, or testing when requested by the Company, will be subject to disciplinary action, which may be immediate termination. When the Company has reason to believe the employee is violating this policy, the employee may be suspended immediately pending investigation.

7. **New Hires** — All new hires and re-hires of regular full-time or part-time employees may be required to take a urine or other medical test and to agree in writing to allow the results of those tests to be furnished to and used by the Company. Those persons who do not pass such test(s) shall not be employed.

8. **Notification of Law Enforcement Agencies and Other Actions** — Other actions, such as notification of law enforcement agencies, may be taken in regard to an employee violating this policy at the Company's discretion as it deems appropriate.

## AUTHORIZATION FOR TESTING

I, [name of employee], hereby give my voluntary consent for [name of company], [name of clinic], and other persons or entities acting for or with them, (1) to collect blood and urine samples from me and to test for the presence of alcohol, drugs, and controlled substances; and (2) to conduct other medical tests.

_____        _____
[Name of employee]                 [Date]

## AUTHORIZATION FOR RELEASE AND USE OF TESTING INFORMATION

I, [name of employee], hereby authorize [name of clinic], to release to [name of company], its Manager of Employee Relations and designees, all results of the alcohol, drug, and/or controlled substances tests and medical examinations performed on me by [name of clinic]. I further authorize [name of company] and its management to communicate this information internally as it deems appropriate and to use this information for any purpose, including — but not limited to — evaluating whether or not to employ me or terminate my employment. [Name of clinic] is authorized to communicate this information at any time until [specific date]. Once such information is communicated, [name of company] and its employees and agents are authorized to use it at any time thereafter.

I understand that I have the right to receive a copy of this Authorization.

_____        _____
[Name of employee]                 [Date]

# Acknowledgments

The author wishes to acknowledge the contributions of Dr. J. Michael Walsh, Chief, Clinical and Behavioral Pharmacology Branch, National Institute on Drug Abuse (NIDA) and the usefulness of resources published by Dr. Walsh and his colleagues at NIDA, especially Dr. Richard L. Hawks.

Other extremely helpful source material included the publication "Alcohol & Drugs in the Workplace: Costs, Controls, and Controversies," a special report of the Bureau of National Affairs, and the March 17, 1986, *Time* article "Battling the Enemy Within." Both are cited in the section entitled "Other Reference Sources," which includes numerous other sources of information which were used for the research and in the preparation of this publication.

The author appreciates the significant contributions of Jan Peter Ozga, Director of the Clearinghouse on Business Coalitions for Health Action; James C. Paras and Jonathan V. Holtzman of the law firm of Morrison and Foerster in San Francisco; and John C. Fox of the law firm of Paul, Hastings, Janofsky, and Walker in Washington, D.C. Nancy L. Abell and Paul W. Cane, Jr. of the Los Angeles office of Paul, Hastings, Janofsky and Walker provided the sample company policy statement and authorizations in Appendix E and their contributions also are very much appreciated.

Finally, the author's thanks and appreciation are extended to Valerie A. Greene, his assistant, for her able assistance.